Estranged Lives
A Living Guide for Coping with Estrangement

GRACE MAIN

Copyright © 2025 Grace Main

All rights reserved.

FOREWORD

When someone you love becomes a stranger the silence can feel unbearable. Estranged Lives is a compassionate deeply honest guide for anyone grieving the loss of a family relationship especially parents estranged from their adult children through gentle reflection personal stories and emotional wisdom Grace Main walks you through the pain of abandonment the weight of unanswered questions and the slow process of healing. She explores how to release guilt reclaim self-worth and build a meaningful life beyond estrangement this short, yet powerful guide reminds you are not alone in your sorrow you are not broken you are allowed to move forward even without closure with soft strength estranged lives helps you grieve what was accept what is and choose peace anyway. For those navigating invisible grief this book is not just comfort it's company.

Reflection / Journal

"Sometimes the strongest thing you can do is let go." – Unknown

"Grief is not a disorder, a disease or a sign of weakness. It is an emotional, physical and spiritual necessity." – Earl Grollman

Chapter 1 the beginning of the separation

The beginning of a family estrangement it's not just a moment it's a series of realizations that chip away at your heart it takes everything you have to stay strong and not get dragged down you hold on for dear life replaying what happened and wondering if it's your fault this is one of the most exhausting experiences you will ever live through grieving someone who is still alive a child a sibling a parent a friend one day they're part of your world the next you're blocked ignored left without explanation you keep hoping it shall be a phase just a misunderstanding. You replay old conversations and grasp for answers that never come in time you stop expecting then you stop hoping then you learn something painful and true you can miss someone and still move forward without them. Estrangement shakes your identity it leaves you questioning your worth but this chapter marks not just the loss it marks the start of your becoming you are not who you were before the silence but you are still here still worthy still becoming.

Reflection / Journal

When did I first feel the shift in this relationship, and how did it affect me?

_____
_____
_____
_____
_____
_____
_____
_____
_____
_____
_____
_____
_____
_____
_____
_____
_____
_____
_____
_____
_____
_____
_____

"The wound is the place where the Light enters you." – Rumi

Chapter 2

Looking at yourself in the mirror.

There comes a point in estrangement when you stop asking why did they leave? and start asking who am I now? That's when the healing begins after the heartbreak the silence and the waiting you're left with one person yourself you walk into the bathroom look into the mirror and face someone you don't quite recognize any more a version of yourself changed by grief you begin to wonder am I broken am I to blame can I survive this and the answer is yes you can.

The influence of the past.

Many of us were raised without the love we needed we may have come from silence criticism or abandonment and carry those wounds into our own parenting or relationships so we tried harder loved deeper gave more but estrangement still came and now the person staring back at you in the mirror feels lost, but she is not broken she is the beginning of something new.

Reflection / Journal

Who am I becoming now that I've been changed by this experience?

_____
_____
_____
_____
_____
_____
_____
_____
_____
_____
_____
_____
_____
_____
_____
_____
_____
_____
_____
_____
_____
_____

"Healing doesn't mean the damage never existed. It means the damage no longer controls your life." – Akshay Dubey

Ask yourself what do you see when I look at myself now what am I still carrying that I can choose to lay down can I treat myself the same grace I gave to others you deserve your own compassion.

Chapter 3 adult child estrangement

Estrangement one from a child is a unique kind of grief it's not loud or public there's no funeral no ceremony no final good bye just silence the child you carried fed held cheered for the one you loved with your entire being become someone who won't return your call who walks past you like he's stranger who rewrites history without your voice it feels like a death you're not allowed to grieve you begin to doubt everything was I too strict too soft too much did I miss the moment when it all turned did I fail you may never get clear answers and that's one of the hardest things of all

The secret grief

You suffer in silence others don't understand they may say you must have been done something.

They'll come around just give it time but you know it's deeper than that and no one sees the thousands of moments small and sacred that made you a parent long before the silence began. You are still a parent.

Reflection ask yourself what pain have I been hiding what truths do I need to honor for myself what love do I still carry?

Reflection / Journal

What did I give as a parent that I want to honor and remember?

_____
_____
_____
_____
_____
_____
_____
_____
_____
_____
_____
_____
_____
_____
_____
_____
_____
_____
_____
_____

"Sometimes the strongest thing you can do is let go." – Unknown
You can grieve and still grow you can miss them and still live.

Chapter 4 silence

Silence has a sound it hums at 2:00 AM it echoes during holidays it waits beside your phone unanswered after estrangement silence becomes your new normal but it's anything but peaceful it's loud in its own way a kind of emotional noise that fills the space where love used to live you checked your phone but the message doesn't come you send a card but there's no reply you try to pretend it doesn't hurt but your body knows and so does your heart.

Living without closure.

This kind of silence is different it's not just quiet it's absence it's rejection wrapped in nothingness it's the kind of loss that leaves no visible wound yet it bleeds every day and yet you wake up you go to work you smile at strangers because life goes on even when a piece of you is missing.

Reflection / Journal

What have I been hoping to hear, and how do I begin healing without it?

"You are not a problem to be solved. You are a person to be loved." – Unknown

Ask yourself what does silence say to me what have I been hoping it might one day break open to reveal what would it mean to make peace with not knowing you are still here you are still whole even in the quiet.

Chapter 5 the start of letting go

Letting go is not an event it's a process a slow and painful shift from holding on to hope to holding onto yourself at first it feels like giving up you think if I stop hoping will I stop loving but letting go is not the end of love it's the beginning of self-respect it's choosing to stop waiting for someone who may never return it's choosing to live even with an open wound.

You don't let go because you stopped caring to let go because you can't keep breaking yourself to hold on to someone who already left.

The first small steps.

Letting go doesn't have to be dramatic it can start small not checking your phone for them not sending one more message just in case not rearranging your joy to leave a seat open letting go can feel like loss but it's also freedom.

Reflection / Journal

What am I holding onto that is holding me back?

"Grief is not a disorder, a disease or a sign of weakness. It is an emotional, physical and spiritual necessity." – Earl Grollman
ask yourself

What am I still clinging to?

What part of myself wants to be free if I wasn't waiting for them? What would I do next letting go is in forgetting it's choosing to live?

Chapter 6 rebuilding a life of your own

After the silence after the heartbreak after the letting go, what now?

This is the question that steers you down and for the first time the answer doesn't involve them this part of the journey is about you rebuilding a life of your own means waking up and asking what do I need today not what might they want not what will make them come back but you.

You begin to take small steps making your home feel safe again enjoying meals that nourish your spirit saying yes to laughter saying no to guilt you begin to see that your life because we value not as a parent partner or role but as a person.

You are still here.

You survived you endured now you're rebuilding not just what was lost but what was always waiting to be discovered.

Reflection / Journal

What small daily acts can help me feel grounded and whole again?

"Closure isn't something they give you. It's something you find in yourself." – Grace Main

Ask yourself what have I put off in my life while waiting for someone else what does peace look like on my terms?

Who am I when I belong to myself?

This is your life and it's not too late to live it.

Chapter 7 are you still a parent

Estrangement doesn't erase the years it doesn't unlock the cradles it doesn't undo the bedtime stories the scrape knees or the whispered I love you in the dark you are still a parent even if your child no longer calls you one the loss can feel like a death without a body a grief that others don't understand but you remember and your love didn't disappear just because theirs did.

Invisible but real.

People may not understand they may say the wrong things or nothing at all but deep inside you know what you gave what you carried what you tried to fix even when it wasn't yours to fix estrangement doesn't define your parenting your love does you can still be proud of the heart you brought to the role even if they don't see it you do.

Reflection / Journal

How do I define myself as a parent, regardless of my child's absence?

_____
_____
_____
_____
_____
_____
_____
_____
_____
_____
_____
_____
_____
_____
_____
_____
_____
_____
_____

"Healing doesn't mean the damage never existed. It means the damage no longer controls your life." – Akshay Dubey

Ask yourself

How have I remained present even in absence? What truths do I hold about the parent I was? What do I want to believe about myself now? You are still a parent and you still matter.

Chapter 8 are you still a parent

Estrangement is always isolating but when the people around you don't understand or worse judge it deepens the wound you hear things like what did you do they'll come back that would never happen in my family.

And behind those words is the suggestion you must be the problem.

But they didn't live your story they don't know the complexity they don't see the years of effort the tears behind closed doors or the pain of being erased by someone's you still love.

You don't owe anyone your story.

Not everyone deserves access to your pain you don't have to explain your grief to make it real you don't need to convince anyone to validate your loss

find those who can hold space without fixing
blaming or comparing you deserve to be believed
nor questioned.

Reflection / Journal

Who understands me, and what boundaries protect my healing?

"Healing doesn't mean the damage never existed. It means the damage no longer controls your life." – Akshay Dubey

Ask yourself

Who truly sees me as I am?

Who makes my pain feel heavier?

What boundaries protect my healing?

You are not here to prove yourself to the world you are here to heal and to be held with care.

Chapter 9

Rebuilding trust in yourself.

Estrangement doesn't just damage relationships it damages your confidence in your own reality you begin to wonder was I really a good parent was it all my fault.

Did I imagine the love we once shared you start to doubt your instincts your memories even your worth but here's the truth you are not the unreliable narrator of your life.

You lived it.

You remember what you gave.

You know how hard you tried.

You don't need to be perfect to be believed.

Maybe you made mistakes all parents do maybe you've said things you regret all humans do.

But that doesn't mean you caused this alone.

And it doesn't mean you don't deserve peace.

Rebuilding trust in yourself starts with compassion the truth with letting go of the shame that doesn't belong to you.

Reflection / Journal

What do I know to be true about myself that no one can take away?

"Closure isn't something they give you. It's something you find in yourself." – Grace Main

Ask yourself

What parts of my story have I silenced to protect others?

What do I know deep down that I've been afraid to claim?

What would trusting myself again feel like you are not the problem you are the path forward?

Chapter 10

Redefining what family means.

Once family meant blood it meant loyalty holiday shared names and stories but estrangement forces a new definition because when those closest to you become strangers or choose to leave you begin to ask what is family really and the answer is this.

Family is who sees you stays with you loves you by choice not obligation.

Grieving the myth.

There's a myth that family always comes through that they forgive that they protect that they say but many of us learn the hard way family can also hurt judge abandon and rewrite the truth it's OK to grieve what you were taught family would be and then it's OK to redefine it.

Choosing your people.

Family can now mean a friend who checks in without being asked a pet who waits by the door a support group where you're not too much yourself finally loving you.

Reflection / Journal

Who in my life today shows up for me with love and consistency?

_____
_____
_____
_____
_____
_____
_____
_____
_____
_____
_____
_____
_____
_____
_____
_____
_____
_____
_____
_____
_____
_____
_____
_____
_____
_____

"Closure isn't something they give you. It's something you find in "Sometimes the strongest thing you can do is let go." – Unknown

Ask yourself

What does family mean to me now?

Who feels like home?

Who honors my truth?

You get to choose who you call family now and you deserve to feel safe in that choice.

Chapter 11

Loving without closure.

Sometimes love doesn't end with a goodbye it ends with a slow fade a silence a sudden cut off and yet your love doesn't disappear it lingers you still wonder about them still hope they're OK still remember their laugh they're habits the way once leaned on you but you're left without an explanation without resolution without closure.

Closure isn't always possible.

We're told that healing requires closure but not all stories and neatly sometimes people leave and you never know why sometimes the truth never comes and waiting foreclosure can keep you stuck real healing doesn't come from them it comes from the decision to stop holding your breath.

Loving from afar.

You can still love them without letting that love hurt you can keep the good memories without reopening the wounds you can grieve remember release.

Reflection / Journal

What love do I still carry, and how can I hold it gently without pain?

_____
_____
_____
_____
_____
_____
_____
_____
_____
_____
_____
_____
_____
_____
_____
_____
_____
_____
_____
_____
_____
_____
_____

"Closure isn't something they give you. It's something you find in yourself." – Grace Main

Ask yourself

What am I still hoping they'll say?

What would it feel like to stop waiting?

Can I love without needing to hold on?

Closure isn't a door they close it's peace you choose.

Chapter 12 forgiveness on your own terms

Forgiveness is often misunderstood it's not forgetting it's not excusing it's not saying it's OK forgiveness when you choose it is for you not for them it's saying I will not carry this bitterness forever it's saying I deserve peace more than I deserve answers it's saying I choose myself over the wound.

You don't have to forgive to heal some people find freedom and forgiveness others find it in setting boundaries and never looking back both are valid forgiveness is not a requirement it's an option your option and you don't owe it to any one especially not the person who refuses to see your pain.

Forgiving yourself.

Sometimes the hardest person to forgive is you carry the guilt the what ifs the self-doubt but you are not perfect you were never meant to be you were doing your best.

Reflection / Journal

What would it look like to stop carrying guilt that isn't mine?

"Closure isn't something they give you. It's something you find in yourself." – Grace Main

Ask yourself

What does forgiveness look like for me not for them have I been punishing myself more than healing myself?

What would it feel like to release what I can't control?

You get to define your path you get to choose your peace.

Chapter 13 when hope changes shape

In the beginning hope sounds like reunion you imagine their voice again their presence a text an apology you hold on to the hope that they'll come back but as time passes hope starts to hurt it keeps you tethered to a moment that may never arrive it becomes a weight instead of a lifeline and then something shifts you realize hope doesn't have to die it can change.

A different kind of hope instead of hoping they'll return hope that you can return to yourself instead of hoping for their love hope for peace within your own heart instead of hoping they'll change hope for the strength to move forward even if they don't hope becomes less about them and more about you

This is not giving up.

Letting go of one version of hope doesn't mean you've stopped caring it means you're clearing space for something better a life that doesn't revolve around someone else's absence.

Reflection / Journal

What kind of hope supports my healing today?

_____
_____
_____
_____
_____
_____
_____
_____
_____
_____
_____
_____
_____
_____
_____
_____
_____
_____
_____
_____
_____
_____
_____

"The wound is the place where the Light enters you." – Rumi

What hope have I outgrown?

What New Hope can I hold?

Can I honor my heart and still move forward?

Hope is still yours. Just shaped differently now

Chapter 14 finding meaning in the mess

Estrangement feels like chaos there's no clean ending no clear beginning just pain confusion and silence you ask yourself why did this happen what does it mean but sometimes there's no satisfying reason and that's OK because meaning doesn't always come from the past sometimes it comes from the way you carry the present.

What if the meaning is in you.

Maybe the meaning isn't why they laughed maybe the meaning is how you keep going how you find strength and honesty how you learn to love yourself through sorrow you don't need their explanation to find your purpose you don't need a clean story to build a meaningful future.

Reason versus Meaning.

Reasons ask why did this happen.

Meaning as what will I do with what happened you may never understand why they walked away but you can choose how you live in their absence reflection.

Reflection / Journal

What meaning am I creating by choosing to keep going?

"You are not a problem to be solved. You are a person to be loved." – Unknown

Ask yourself

What meaning can I create from my survival how has this changed me in painful but almost powerful ways?

You are not just what happened to you are what you become.

Chapter 15 returning to yourself

Estrangement doesn't just take someone from your life it can take you from yourself you begin to forget who you were before the grief you shrink you second guess you stop trusting your joy you define yourself by the silence the blame the pain but now something inside you is calling it's time to come home to you.

Who were you before the silence before they left you were more than someone's parents sibling or partner you were someone with dreams with a voice with a full beating heart that person is still here waiting healing becoming.

Reclaiming yourself coming back to yourself means listening to your needs.

Releasing the roles that no longer fit.

Writing a new story one that centers you.

It means treating yourself with the care you gave to everyone else.

Reflection / Journal

What parts of myself have I lost—and which ones am I ready to reclaim?

_____
_____
_____
_____
_____
_____
_____
_____
_____
_____
_____
_____
_____
_____
_____
_____
_____
_____
_____
_____

"Sometimes the strongest thing you can do is let go." – Unknown

Ask yourself

Who am I apart from what I've lost what have I silenced that I want to reclaim?

What kind of life would honor my truth?

You are not broken you are still becoming and you are worth coming home too.

Chapter 16

The life you still deserve.

You've survived the silence you've grieved question and broken open and now something gentler as possible not because the pain is gone but because your life is still yours you still deserve joy you still deserve peace you still deserve a future that feels like you.

More than survival.

You've done the hardest part you've endured but now is the time to build to plant something beautiful in the soil of all you've lost not for anyone else for you are allowed to live fully even without their approval even without their presence.

Let this life be yours.

This chapter isn't about waiting it's about creating it's the sound of your own voice returning the feel of your breath in your chest the quiet joy of life reclaimed.

Reflection / Journal

What kind of life do I long to live from this point forward?

"You don't have to rebuild a relationship with everyone you've forgiven." – Unknown

Ask yourself

What kind of life do I still long for?

What would it mean to choose that life without guilt?

You are not what they left behind.

You are what rises anyway.

Chapter 17

A letter to you

Dear reader if no one else has said it let me say it now I see you.

I see the silence you sit with the grief you carry quietly the way you question your worth in the dark the way you've kept going even without understanding why they left you are not weak for loving you are not broken because they walked away you are not alone in this pain you survived A grief most people don't even recognize you've lost someone who's still alive and still live with that ache every day.

But still you rise you rise when you make your

coffee in the morning he rise when you take a walk just to feel your feet you rise when you cry and then still keep moving That is strength that is you this book isn't an answer it's a companion a mirror a reminder that your story doesn't end here you're not just someone who's been hurt you are someone who is healing and you're healing is your legacy.

With you always,

Grace

Reflection / Journal

What would I say to myself, if I were offering compassion and truth?

Introduction

If you're reading this you might be feeling alone maybe someone you love has cut you off without answers without closure I've lived that pain and I wrote this for you not as a therapist not as a perfect parent but as someone who knows the silence sorrow and the strength it takes to keep living.

Back Cover

Grace Main as a mother writer and survivor of multiple family estrangements her journey through grief healing and self-reinvention led her to write a strange lives a living guide born from personal pain and the desire to help others feel seen and supported grace writes with raw honesty and compassion offering strength to those rebuilding their lives after deep emotional loss she lives in Massachusetts and finds peace and walking riding and sharing hope with others on the path toward healing

Printed in Dunstable, United Kingdom